D0046338

IRVINE VALLEY COLLEGE LIBRARY

Cambridge English Readers

Level 4

Series editor: Philip Prowse

Nothing but the Truth

George Kershaw

CAMBRIDGE
UNIVERSITY PRESS

CAMBRIDGE UNIVERSITY PRESS
Cambridge, New York, Melbourne, Madrid, Cape Town, Singapore, São Paulo

Cambridge University Press
The Edinburgh Building, Cambridge CB2 2RU, UK

www.cambridge.org
Information on this title: www.cambridge.org/9780521656238

© Cambridge University Press 1999

This publication is in copyright. Subject to statutory exception
and to the provisions of relevant collective licensing agreements,
no reproduction of any part may take place without the written
permission of Cambridge University Press.

First published 1999
10th printing 2005

Printed in the United Kingdom at the University Press, Cambridge

A catalogue record for this publication is available from the British Library

ISBN-13 978-0-521-65623-8 paperback
ISBN-10 0-521-65623-0 paperback

For my daughter, Mary.

No character in this work is based on any person living or dead. Any resemblance
to an actual person or situation is purely accidental.

Contents

Characters

Hu Jian Ming: from China, a seventeen-year-old female student at the Bangkok International Academy.

Hu An Yuan: Hu's father, an engineer for a Chinese oil company. He manages their Bangkok office.

Wang Xue Mei: Hu's mother.

Marwa Marlati: from Iran.

Thomas Kuhlauf: from Germany.

Yoshiko Ito: from Japan.

Sean Payne: half Thai, half American.

John Truman: from America.

students at the Bangkok International Academy.

Verity Truman: John's mother, head of Upper School at the Academy.

Declan Stanyer: Hu's English teacher.

Aubrey Grisman: the principal of the Academy.

David Riding: the school counsellor.

Mrs Patel: the music teacher.

Miss Paula: the librarian.

Mr Rodriguez: the biology teacher.

Wiwat Phalavadhana: an important official.

Lao Mao: Hu's cat.

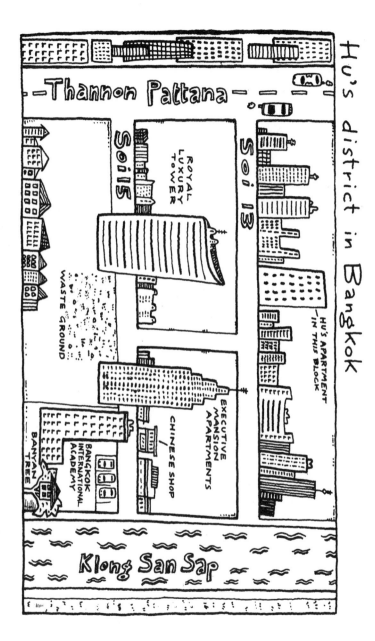

Thailand and the Khao Yai National Park

Chapter 1   *Dawn in Bangkok*

Hu decided to get up. She couldn't sleep. The first bird of the Bangkok dawn, the cuckoo, started its noisy, morning cry, '*Gow-wow! Gow-wow!* Get up! Get up!' Hu could hear the growing noise of the early morning traffic. It was not yet six o'clock.

It was impossible to sleep. She walked over to her window and opened it. The noise and the smell of the big city washed over her. It was still dark. It was a cool January morning, the first day of the spring term.

Hu looked out of the window. The newspaper man arrived on his motorbike and gave his parcel of newspapers to the man at the entrance of the apartment block. The two men laughed, and then the newspaper man waved and drove noisily away to the next apartment block in the Soi, the next street. There was light in the sky now, a soft orange light in the grey dawn.

It was always difficult to sleep the night before the new term, but this time it was even harder. Hu was excited. She would see Marwa and Thomas and Yoshiko again, and that was exciting. She would do less housework and more school work, and that was exciting too.

*   *   *

Hu was seventeen and a good student. She studied at the Bangkok International Academy, an international school for the children of foreign people working in Thailand. It was expensive, but the Chinese oil company, where her father worked, helped her family to pay for her education. She had to study very hard, and all the classes – except her Thai language class – were in English. Hu loved English. Her father wanted her to become a doctor. Her mother said she didn't mind what Hu wanted as long as Hu was happy. But Hu wasn't sure if she wanted to be a doctor, or that she would get good enough results to go to medical school.

Hu liked to work hard, but she was worried about her studies, about her English exam. Today Mr Stanyer, her English teacher, would give out the results of last term's English test. Hu knew she had problems with her English, but she didn't know what the problems were. She loved English – or she *had* loved English until she started with Mr Stanyer last term – and she thought she was good at English. Her classmates thought she was good at English too. She helped Marwa with her English homework sometimes, but then Marwa got better results than Hu. Better results with *her* work!

Hu didn't understand. Mr Stanyer seemed to like her, he always smiled at her. But at the end of last term, after the test, he had asked her to stay after class.

'Come here and sit down,' Mr Stanyer said. Hu sat at his desk in the empty classroom, facing her teacher.

'How was the test, Hu Jian Ming?' asked Mr Stanyer.

'OK, Mr Stanyer. I think I did quite well,' said Hu.

'I hope so. Your father has great hopes for you. He works for an oil company, doesn't he?' Mr Stanyer smiled and looked Hu in the eye.

'He's an engineer with a Chinese oil company.' Hu felt

uncomfortable.

'He wants you to take the International Baccalaureate, the IB, doesn't he?' Mr Stanyer continued with questions.

'Well, you must get better results next term. This is just a test, but next term we have the real exam. Then we decide if you can start the IB programme,' said Mr Stanyer.

'Yes, Mr Stanyer.' She noticed Mr Stanyer was sweating, although the classroom was cool.

Mr Stanyer smiled and put his hands on his bald head. 'Perhaps you should do some extra work on your English. Think about it over the holiday.'

*   *   *

'Oh!' said Hu. Her cat, Lao Mao, had jumped suddenly into her room through the open window, surprising her. 'Stupid cat!' said Hu as she picked up Lao Mao. Hu loved animals, she loved nature. Her home city, Wu Xi, was in beautiful countryside, with lakes and low hills in the distance. When Hu's family had to leave China and come to Thailand so that Hu's father could work for his oil company in Bangkok, her mother and father allowed her to bring one thing to remind her of home. Hu chose to bring Lao Mao. Hu liked to talk to him when she was sad, or worried, or feeling a long way from home. Very quietly, she explained her problems with her results for her English studies to the cat.

'If I fail my English test, what can I do?' whispered Hu. Lao Mao said nothing. The noisy cuckoo sang back across the waking city: '*Gow-wow! Gow-wow!*'

Hu looked over the apartment blocks to the raised motorway carrying traffic over the city, and the private gardens of the few remaining houses. Bangkok. She missed her own country very much. The sun was rising over the block opposite hers like a big, wet, orange ball. A man in yellow clothes, a Buddhist monk, was walking up the road asking for food. A big Mercedes car came round to the front gate. 'Probably a businessman going to the airport,' thought Hu.

Hu yawned. What would she do?

Something caught her eye in the Soi below. A very large orange and black animal, a squirrel, was running along an electricity line over the Soi. Electricity lines ran across the Soi in a hundred different directions, meeting at the posts at the sides of the street in big balls. Hu thought these balls of electricity lines looked like spaghetti. The squirrels used the electricity lines like motorways, running to and from whatever important business squirrels have to do. Hu looked towards the raised motorway in the distance. All the cars were stopped even now, at half past six in the morning. Another Bangkok traffic jam. Hu's eyes followed the racing squirrel along the line and down into another garden.

There was a knock at the door.

'Jian Ming! Come on, my love. It's a school day today.'

That was her father. He was usually out of bed first. He worked very hard.

'I'm out of bed, father. I'm coming. Don't worry.'

'Don't worry,' thought Hu. 'My father mustn't worry,' she told Lao Mao, her cat. 'He works too hard.'

Lao Mao said nothing. He didn't care.

Chapter 2   *New term, old friends*

Hu walked up the narrow Soi to school. She felt happy and excited. The early morning sun was bright. It almost hurt her eyes. It was cool and the skies were blue and clear.

There were street restaurants which had small tables and tiny plastic chairs on the pavements. Hu stepped into the road as she walked past them. City workers sat and ate bowls of *khao dhom*, a thick rice soup. They wore their office clothes, and they ate quickly, talking and laughing at the same time. The shop opposite the school was full of students from the international school in their blue uniforms. They were buying drinks and snacks. Some of them had spent two hours or more fighting their way through the Bangkok traffic jams to get to school.

There was a loud noise as a boat raced down the *klong*, the canal at the end of the Soi. Water flew into the air. The smell of the dirty water made Hu feel sick for a moment. 'Everybody is trying to get to work or to school. Everyone is busy, hurrying,' thought Hu. It filled her with excitement.

She walked past the building workers' dark, small homes. They were building another expensive apartment building for rich people to live in, but the building workers lived in their own tiny, dark city. They had built their small world on some waste ground between two tall new buildings, the Royal Luxury Tower and Executive Mansion Apartments. Their homes were made out of old sheets of metal, pieces of wood and useful bits of rubbish. Babies were crying, women were washing clothes, themselves, and children. Hu could see a television, men playing cards, chickens looking for food in the dirt and a small dog asleep in the middle of all the noise. Women and men were walking in silence from their crowded homes to their work. Hu tried to look into their sad, dark eyes. They would breathe and eat the dirt all the long working day, and often late into the night. Hu tried to smile at them but they didn't smile back.

It was wonderful for Hu to see her friends again. They crowded together at the entrance to the school. They were all trying to tell the others what they had been doing during the holidays at once. Thomas Kuhlauf had been home to Germany for Christmas. He had a special German cake, called a stollen. He gave Hu and Marwa and Yoshiko a piece each while they waited for the bell for the beginning of school.

They were still eating Thomas' wonderful cake as they went into the school hall.

Hu found herself sitting next to a new student. He was tall and had blond hair. He had a friendly face, with quick eyes and a ready smile.

'Hi! I'm John Truman from the USA. This is my first day here. What's your name?' said the stranger, smiling. He very politely offered Hu his hand. Hu was surprised, but she smiled and shook his hand.

'I'm Hu. From China ... Hu Jian Ming. Your first day?'

'Shhhh!' said Marwa, who was sitting on her other side. 'Mr Grisman! Mustn't talk!'

The school principal, Mr Grisman, walked on to stage and raised his hands to tell the whole school to be quiet and listen. He was tall and had grey hair. He was wearing dark clothes and a very serious expression. Hu thought he looked silly. He stared at them importantly until there was silence, and then he smiled and said:

'Welcome! Welcome! Happy New Year! And welcome to a new year at the Bangkok International Academy...'

'It's not my new year yet, it's not the Chinese New Year until next month. It's not the Thai New Year until April. It's not Marwa's or Yoshiko's either,' thought Hu. She stopped listening.

She looked at the teachers sitting behind Mr Grisman on the stage. Mr Stanyer, her English teacher, was yawning. He was very sun-tanned. Mr Riding, the school counsellor, looked like a sleeping animal, until his eyes suddenly opened and slowly stared around the hall. Mrs Patel, the music teacher, was looking very pleased with life. She was wearing a lovely new sari, her traditional Indian dress. Where was Dr Nyondo, the head of Upper School?

There was a new woman. She was tall and about forty years old. She sat very straight. She had blond hair and a kind, intelligent face.

'... And as Dr Nyondo has left us to take up the position of principal of a high school in Australia, it is my pleasure ...' Mr Grisman looked round at the woman who stood up. '... My great pleasure to introduce Mrs Verity Truman as the new head of Upper School.'

'That's my mother!' said John.

'Shhh!' said Marwa. 'Mustn't talk!'

But they did, as quietly as they could. Hu and John made friends while his mother made a short speech.

John was from Chicago, Illinois. He had one sister,

Mary, who was in the fifth year. His father was a lawyer with a multinational company. John's father was now working in the Bangkok headquarters of his company, and working very long hours.

'My father's like that!' said Hu. 'I don't see much of him. I go to bed before he comes home in the evening. We don't have much time to talk even in the mornings.'

'What does he do?' asked John.

Hu told him that her father worked as an engineer for a Chinese oil company, managing the company's Bangkok office and projects in Eastern Thailand. And that her mother looked after small children at a kindergarten in the mornings and sometimes did baby-sitting at night. She told him that she had a pet cat called Lao Mao and that she liked music . . . and all kinds of things.

Mr Grisman was still talking. He invited Mrs Patel to talk to the school about the new school show. It was a musical called 'The Wizard of Oz'. Mrs Patel was going to hold auditions on Friday after school.

'What does "auditions" mean?' whispered Hu to John.

'You have to try out acting and singing in front of the people organising the show. If you're good, they give you a part. Do you sing, Hu?' asked John.

Hu was excited. 'I love singing. I can act too. I . . .'

'Shhh!' said Marwa. Mrs Patel looked angrily at Hu and John. Hu's face went red with embarrassment.

* * *

The first day passed happily and quickly. Hu was happy to be back among her friends and studying again after the holidays.

14

As Hu went into her last class, a Thai language class, her Thai teacher, Khun Naraporn, handed her a note. It was from Mr Stanyer, her English teacher. It read:

Please see me after class today. I want to discuss your English results with you.
D. S.

Marwa watched her read the note.

'Are you OK?' Marwa asked.

Hu passed her the note.

'Miss Hu! Please pay attention! Today we are going to study the traditions of the Thai New Year,' said Khun Naraporn.

'Oh dear!' thought Hu. She was very worried. She was sure the note was bad news. What was Mr Stanyer going to say? She tried to concentrate on her Thai lesson.

Chapter 3   *Sharing troubles*

'But, Mr Stanyer? Forty-six per cent?'

'It's not good, Hu. It's not good.' Mr Stanyer was shaking his head.

'But, really, I . . .' Hu was close to tears.

'Listen!' said Mr Stanyer, leaning forward across the desk. His big red face was close to Hu's. He picked up Hu's writing test. 'Here's your work!'

He threw it across the desk at Hu. Hu thought this was very rude. As she collected the papers together, she knew her feelings would show in her face. She had worked hard on the essay and now it was covered in red ink.

'OK, Hu,' said Mr Stanyer. He smiled. Hu didn't like his smile. He tried to laugh and leant back in his chair and put his hands on his bald head. The classroom was air-conditioned, almost too cool, but there were dark marks under his arms. 'You're a good kid, a *bright* kid. Your father wants you to be a doctor, right?'

'Yes, but . . .' Hu said.

'Yes, but!' Mr Stanyer moved forward suddenly hitting his hands on the desk between them.

'YES BUT!' he repeated in a loud voice to scare her. Then he remembered to smile. 'But your results have got to improve. It's only six weeks until the exams for the IB, the International Baccalaureate programme. Forty-six per cent is a fail. You can't be a doctor unless you get the IB.'

He could see Hu was going to cry. He pushed his chair back and stood up. He took a handkerchief from his pocket and wiped his forehead. He tried a new voice, a voice like a child asking their mother for a sweet.

'Hu, we can work on this. Together.' Mr Stanyer walked round the desk and slowly sat down in the chair next to Hu. He smelled of sweat. He put his arm on the back of Hu's chair. Hu sat as far forward as she could and looked at the desk. She was trying not to cry, trying not to smell Mr Stanyer's fat smell.

'It's a question of work. You're intelligent.' Hu looked at the desk. 'You work hard, Chinese people work hard,' said Mr Stanyer, laughing. 'Maybe I can help you, Hu?'

Hu tried to look at him. He was smiling his biggest, his most sugary smile.

'You need some extra lessons. Private lessons. One-to-one. After class. We can work on this exam preparation together.'

'You would give me lessons?' asked Hu. Mr Stanyer stood up and walked back to his own seat opposite her.

'Sure. Well, not exactly *give* you lessons. I mean, you'd have to pay.'

'I don't have any money, Mr Stanyer. How can I pay?' asked Hu.

'Hey! Your father's an oil engineer. You should talk to him!'

'But I can't tell ...' Hu started to say, but she stopped. Now she stood up. She was very angry. She looked down at Mr Stanyer.

'I shall have to discuss this with my father.' She walked to the door without looking back.

'Sure!' Mr Stanyer called after her. 'Talk to your father. But Hu, those results have got to improve!'

Hu didn't start crying until she was outside the classroom.

*　　*　　*

There is a small wooden house in a banyan tree in the south corner of the school playing field, near the *klong*. The *klong* smell is very bad there, but after school it is a place you can sit alone.

Hu climbed in and threw herself into a broken car seat. She put her head in her hands and cried. She couldn't go home like this.

Her father wanted her to be a doctor. And now she was getting bad results. Hu's shoulders shook as she cried.

But she still didn't understand. All her other results were good or very good. In music and in drama she was, her teachers said, a 'star'. She dried her eyes.

Hu looked up. A face appeared in the entrance to the tree house.

'Can I come in?' said the face. It was her new friend, John Truman. As he said this, another face appeared. It was a small blond girl.

'This is my sister, Mary,' John said.

'Hi!' said Mary as the two pulled themselves into the tree house.

'This is Hu Jian Ming, Mary. And she doesn't look very happy,' John said.

'Hi Mary! Hi John!' Hu tried to look happy. 'What are you doing here?'

'Waiting for mother,' said Mary. 'She's at a teachers' meeting.'

'What's that?' asked John, pointing at Hu's hand.

Hu had not realised. Her English essay was now a small ball in her hand. She was so angry. She threw the essay to John.

John opened it out.

'That,' said Hu, 'is my English essay. My rubbish essay. My forty-six per cent essay. My failed essay. My ...' She stopped because she thought she was going to cry again.

John tried to read the essay.

'Hey, this is good,' said John. 'But I've never seen so much red ink.'

John read from the essay: ' "Wu Xi, My Home Town. The beautiful sailing boats, their red sails full, moved slowly over the mirror-like surface of the lakes." Wow! You can write! Is this where you live?'

'My father was working in Beijing before we came here. But I was born in Wu Xi. It is my home. My grandmother still lives there, and my mother's family. At our new year, we used to go there ...'

' "The friendly hills gather round the metal-smooth lakes as the skies turn pink," ' John read. 'This is good! When can I go there?'

'My teacher doesn't like it,' said Hu, sadly.

' "Did ..." I can't read his writing ... "you copy this from a guide book?" Huh. I don't think this guy likes you, Hu.'

'I don't know. He's always looking at me in class.' Hu was confused.

John laughed and then looked serious.

'Forty-six per cent isn't very good. I hope this wasn't a test or something.'

John still had half a bottle of water he had bought at the Chinese shop opposite the school gates, and Hu had some of her morning snack left. The three of them had a little picnic. Hu made John and Mary promise not to tell anybody else, and then she explained her problems to them.

Chapter 4   *To be a star*

The noise in the school restaurant was very loud. Three hundred students were all shouting at once. Three hundred metal trays banged upon the tables, and all the metal forks and spoons and knives banged together at the same time.

'A normal day at the BIA,' shouted Hu as she sat down with Marwa, Yoshiko, Thomas and John.

'What's this?' shouted Thomas, pointing with his fork at a small pool of wet brown stuff.

'Food, Mr Kuhlauf, but not as we know it!' said John.

They all laughed except Marwa. She had her own food from home. Her mother had prepared a rice dish for her. It smelled delicious, and Marwa ate quickly and in silence.

'Are you going to the meeting after school?' asked Thomas. 'It's for the school show, "The Wizard of Oz".'

'Yes, I'm going,' said Hu.

'That awful Melanie Gibson wants to be the star,' said Thomas. 'You know her, she's got long red hair and she sings like a duck! Quack, quack!' he shouted.

'You are unkind, Thomas!' Hu said. 'It's true about her singing though.' She tried to look cross.

'And Sean Payne wants to be the Wizard,' Thomas continued.

'Sean Payne? The one who wasn't allowed to come to school for a while?' asked Yoshiko.

Sean Payne was always in trouble. Once he let out the air

of the tyres on the principal's car. Mr Grisman sent him home and would not let him come back to the school for two weeks.

'That's him. The ugly one with hair like a brush. The one whose father runs a bar. He married one of his dancers, did you know?' said Thomas.

'Thomas Kuhlauf, you talk too much!' said Hu crossly. This time she was really angry. Thomas carried on talking about people who wanted to be in the school show. Hu decided not to listen any more.

John asked as quietly as he could. 'Did you talk to your father about extra English lessons?'

'I can't talk here. It's too noisy. Come to the library.'

*   *   *

Hu often went to the library at lunch time and after school. It was cool. Hu loved to read, and the librarian, Miss Paula, helped her find new and interesting books.

John and Hu found a desk in a corner and talked quietly. Miss Paula let them talk, pretending not to notice. Hu was her favourite student. Hu read more than any other student in the school and often stayed after school to help her. Miss Paula was pleased to see Hu talking to such a good-looking boy. She noticed Hu was looking worried.

'No, I didn't talk to my father. I didn't see him last night or this morning. An important businessman is coming to Bangkok tonight, and my father must prepare for the visit. But . . .'

'Yes?' said John.

'But I don't want to talk to him about it. He worries too much. If he knows about my bad results he'll be angry.

He'll worry about it. And Mr Stanyer wants me to pay for the lessons. My father is not a rich man. I don't know what to do,' Hu explained.

'I've been thinking. Maybe I can help. You show me some more of your work and we can look at it together.'

'But John, that's too kind.'

'Not at all,' said John, smiling. 'Let's do a deal. I have to start Thai lessons, and you already speak Thai . . .'

'I'm not very good,' said Hu.

'Better than me!' said John. 'I'm a complete beginner. I have to wait after school with Mary until my mother has finished. We can study together in here some days.'

Hu thought for a moment. Most afternoons her mother was out doing small jobs to earn some extra money. Hu didn't like to return to the empty flat. And she needed help. John was very kind.

'OK, that's a good idea. Not today, though, there's the meeting about the show. And tomorrow Mr Stanyer wants me to have my first private lesson. But we can start next week.'

'That's agreed then,' said John. 'Oh, and give me your phone number. Then if I have a problem with my homework, I can ring and ask you for help. Or you can ring and ask me. Mine's 250 1972. What's yours?'

'255 1970,' replied Hu without thinking. She felt her face going red. 'But don't phone too late, my parents . . . I mean, I go to bed very early.'

*   *   *

Mrs Patel and John's mother, Mrs Truman, stood on the stage in the main hall with three other teachers.

'Sean? If you would be so good as to stop talking . . .' Mrs Patel began.

'Hi!' shouted Sean, with a silly look on his face.

'For the new students, my name is Mrs Patel, and I am pleased to welcome you all. So many people want to join the show! If we cannot give you a singing part there are many other jobs . . . Mrs Truman' – Mrs Patel gestured to Mrs Truman, who smiled – 'will explain that in a moment. My job is to be musical director. I will train you to sing and, I hope, to act the parts. Mrs Truman will be the producer. Mrs Truman will explain what she is going to be doing, and then I will tell you about how we will choose the actors.'

There were more than thirty students there. Thomas Kuhlauf was very excited, he couldn't keep still. Sean was already talking again. Melanie Gibson was brushing her beautiful red hair. She had changed out of her school uniform and was now wearing a pretty pink dress. 'Quack, quack,' thought Hu. Then she felt guilty.

Mrs Truman explained the job of the producer and all the jobs there were for people who were not singing and acting in the show. 'Making clothes, lighting, painting things, moving things, organising, publicity, tickets . . .' John knew he couldn't sing or act, but he loved painting and organising. He would, he decided, do one of these jobs.

Later they divided into groups. They had two exercises, one singing and one acting exercise.

Hu sat and read the song through. It was easy. She loved to sing. When she was not busy, Hu's mother would teach her to sing. Hu's mother had studied opera before she married. When she was happy, Hu's mother would sing as she did the housework. That was not very often.

The singing went well. Hu sang simply while Mrs Patel played the piano. Some of the other students clapped their hands at the end. John and Thomas clapped hard. Hu was surprised when she saw Sean Payne clapping too, and smiling at her stupidly.

She was even more surprised when she had to act with Sean. Sean loved to make people laugh, and he didn't care if he looked stupid. Often he didn't know when to stop trying to make people laugh, but this time everything went well. He had learned his words and he didn't change anything. He made the other students laugh, and even Mrs Patel and Mrs Truman smiled. Hu felt wonderful. Maybe Sean Payne was not so stupid all the time.

'We think we can decide who will get the major parts straight away,' said Mrs Patel. 'So, I will read a list of people I want to stay behind at five o'clock. The rest of you can come back, please, next Thursday.'

Mrs Patel read out Hu's name. Hu was delighted. She was in the show! And so was Thomas, and Melanie Gibson and ('I don't believe it!' said Hu to John.), Sean Payne.

It was hard to wait to talk to Mrs Patel, Hu was so excited.

'You can have the part of Dorothy,' said Mrs Patel when it was Hu's turn.

'But? But, Dorothy's an American farm girl. I don't look right. I don't look like an American girl. I don't speak like an American. Melanie looks more like Dorothy . . . I . . .'

'Please, Hu!' said Mrs Patel, laughing. 'You sing beautifully. And American girls look just like you and me.'

Mrs Patel put her head back and laughed. 'I mean like me when I was your age. American girls are all different colours and shapes and sizes and ... and you can sing *and* you can act.'

'My mother helped me learn to sing, she studied opera,' Hu said.

'That explains it. And you act very simply and very well. Melanie ...' Mrs Patel paused. She was searching for words.

'Melanie sings like a duck,' thought Hu, but she didn't say anything.

'I think Melanie can be your understudy,' said Mrs Patel, at last.

'Understudy?' Hu didn't understand.

'Yes, someone who can take your place if you are ill. We call this person an "understudy". She will learn your part. If, for some reason, you cannot be in the show, she can be Dorothy.' Mrs Patel looked at Hu, waiting for her reply.

Hu felt unhappy. 'And if I am in the show? If I play Dorothy?'

'There are plenty of other parts for Melanie. Will you take the part?'

*   *   *

Hu waited a few minutes after her talk with Mrs Patel. She waited to know which part Thomas had got. Sean waited with her.

As Melanie left the main hall she turned suddenly and looked Hu in the eyes. Melanie had clearly been crying. Her face was white with anger.

'You! Dorothy!' Melanie laughed. She laughed too loud. 'Hu Jian Ming, I know what you're doing! Just you wait! You'll see! I'll get you!' she was shouting, almost screaming.

'Cool!' said Sean, smiling stupidly.

Chapter 5 *Money worries*

Hu was sitting on the balcony of her apartment. It was evening. She had Lao Mao, the cat, sitting on her knee, but otherwise she was alone. The balcony was full of plants in pots. Her mother loved plants, and filled the apartment and the balcony with growing things. The balcony was so full of plants it was difficult to move. In the family, they called the balcony 'Mother's little jungle'. Hu's father liked to water the plants in the early morning before he went to work. He said it helped him relax.

'Stupid!' said Hu to the cat. Lao Mao said nothing. Hu thought the cat smiled.

Hu was worrying about money.

'Lao Mao, you are lazy, and you don't listen to me. Sit on your own chair!' Hu put the cat on another plastic chair and stood up.

She went to the edge of the balcony and looked across at Bangkok. Bangkok was coming home from work. Bangkok was trying to come home. Hu could see the traffic standing still on the highway. There was the smell of the traffic, a smell of cooking, a smell of dirt, and a smell of plants from the balcony and from the gardens in the Soi below.

'Stupid!' said Hu again, returning to her chair. How could she pay for her extra English lessons? She didn't get a lot of pocket money. Her father was generous but he had said:

'Hu, we have been saving for when you to go to medical school for a long time . . .'

'When?' Hu had thought. '*If* not *when* I go.' But she had said nothing.

'There will be other expenses,' her father had continued. 'You must save too.'

Mr Stanyer had said he would want the money after each lesson, twice a week. Without good results in English, she could not enter the IB programme. Without the IB, medical school was a dream.

It was very quiet in the apartment. Hu's mother was baby-sitting. Hu's mother did small jobs for people, for neighbours in the apartment block and for friends.

Hu's father was a good man, but he didn't understand. He didn't want his wife to work, but he didn't understand how expensive life was in central Bangkok. The oil company gave them a big apartment because he often had to entertain important people from work. But he wasn't a rich man.

Once Hu had offered to do work for money. The answer was no. Her mother was shocked.

'Your education is more important,' she had said. 'One day you will be a doctor. Then you will have money. Concentrate on your studies and your father will be proud of you. Your father cannot let you work . . .'

The doorbell rang, waking Hu from her thoughts. Hu answered it. Marwa stood at the door with a pile of English books in one hand, a plastic box in the other, and a big smile.

'Can I come in?' said Marwa.

'Of course,' said Hu. 'My father's still at work and my mother's baby-sitting.'

It was getting dark in the big empty apartment, so Hu switched the lights on and cleared the dining table. Marwa put the books and the box on the table.

'We've got sweets and we've got English homework!' she said. 'Which do you want first?'

'Sweets!' said Hu. Mrs Marlati, Marwa's mother, was famous for her home-made Iranian sweets. The two friends sat eating sweets and began the homework. Hu thought the homework was easy, but explaining the answers to Marwa made it more interesting.

'Your father always works late,' said Marwa through a mouth full of sweets, 'like my father.'

Hu sighed. 'Yes, he works late. Tonight he must meet an important businessman from the airport. He won't be home before midnight.' She took another sweet and turned the page of the textbook. 'He works too hard, smokes too much and worries too much.'

'My father's the same,' said Marwa.

'I only see him in the morning before school. Even at the weekends he must play golf with important customers. In the morning he wakes me up coughing. He's always tired.'

'But he's an oil engineer. Very important. Very rich!' said Marwa.

Hu thought of her mother's little jobs. 'He's an engineer and he manages the Bangkok office. It's a good job but . . . But I wish he didn't work so hard . . . Mr Stanyer wants us to do up to exercise 3, modal verbs.'

Hu tried to explain modal verbs to Marwa. They talked about their families and ate too many sweets.

Just before half past nine the doorbell and the telephone rang at the same time. Marwa's driver was at the door. He had come to take her home. Hu waved goodbye to Marwa and went to the telephone.

'Hu, sorry. Is it too late? John Truman here.'

'Oh,' said Hu.

'Yeah, good news. They will tell you at school tomorrow. We're going on a field trip to Khao Yai National Park.'

'Khao Yai? We? You mean all of year eleven?' asked Hu.

'Sure. Well, if you want to. It's a geography and biology field trip. Listen: "The oldest and largest of Thailand's national parks . . .," er, sorry I'm reading, ". . . two hundred and fifty wild elephants, twenty-five to thirty tigers, eight hundred species of orchids . . ." '

'That sounds wonderful. But when? How many days? Will it be expensive?' Hu was excited, but she was thinking of money and all the little jobs her mother had to do. She loved animals, flowers and trees. And it would be good to get away from Bangkok. Away from the dirt and the traffic noise, the smells and the hurrying crowds. They never went away at the weekend, her father was always too busy or resting.

'Let's see. Five days, Monday to Friday, first week in March, before the heat gets too bad. Listen . . .?'

'Sorry, John. Sounds great, but I must go!' said Hu and she quickly put the phone down.

Her mother was home. 'Who was that?' she asked quickly.

'John, John Truman,' Hu replied. 'A student from school. An American boy.' Hu's face was going red.

'And what was it about?' her mother asked.

'Oh, nothing. Homework. He wanted to know about, er, geography homework.' Hu didn't like to lie.

'At half past nine in the evening? Do you have time to talk to "American boys" all night? You must study in the evenings if you want to be a doctor. Have you done the washing up?'

Hu quietly went to the kitchen. She did not want to tell her mother about the field trip to Khao Yai National Park. She was thinking about how much money the field trip would cost.

Chapter 6   *Lessons in disappointment*

All the year eleven students met in the video room at lunch time the next day. It was hard to get a seat and some of the taller students had to stand at the back. Mr Rodriguez gave out some information explaining the field trip and the kinds of activities the students would have to do.

Hu looked through the information until she found the part on cost: including everything it was six thousand Baht. Hu laughed sadly, shaking her head. In a low voice she said, 'Stupid!'

Mr Rodriguez suddenly stopped speaking. With all the students in the video room it was getting very hot.

'I'm sorry, Miss Hu, did you have something to tell us?' he asked, drying his big black moustache with a handkerchief.

'No . . . I . . . sorry, Mr Rodriguez.' Hu felt embarrassed. Sean Payne laughed at the back.

'May I continue then?' Hu nodded, her face red with embarrassment. 'Thank you, Miss Hu. Where was I? Yes . . .'

Hu was adding up the cost in her head. It was almost Chinese New Year, an expensive time for Chinese families. All the presents, all the food. Hu knew her family couldn't afford to go home to China for the holiday this year even if Hu's father was not too busy. She had heard her parents arguing about it late one night the week before. There was no way her father could pay for her to go on the field trip.

Then Mr Rodriguez put the lights out and switched on the video. Hu thought it was wonderful. The jungle and the mountains, the cool waterfalls, the many colours of the birds. Hu forgot she was at school.

'Hrrrmmph!' Sean Payne was being an elephant.

Mr Rodriguez stopped the video and switched all the lights on. Sean was standing using his arm as the elephant's trunk, while the boys next to him were laughing.

'Get out, Sean!' shouted Mr Rodriguez. 'You can come and see me at half past three.' Mr Rodriguez touched his moustache with his handkerchief and said something quietly in Spanish. Some of the students at the back of the classroom clapped their hands as Sean left the room.

* * *

Hu found Mr Stanyer's classroom empty when she went there at half past three that afternoon. She waited outside for nearly fifteen minutes until Mr Stanyer came and opened the door. His body touched hers as he pushed past her. He smelled of sweat and tobacco smoke.

'Sorry Hu, I'm a bit late. Had to go to the teachers' room ...' He sat down heavily and opened his desk, taking out a can of cola and some textbooks. He pushed his desk back and put his feet on the desk. He yawned and turned the pages of the textbook.

'So you spoke to your father, Hu?'

'Mr Stanyer, I don't want my father to know about these lessons. He worries about my results. I don't want him to worry. If my results improve, there won't be a problem.'

Mr Stanyer smiled slowly, his hands on his bald head. He laughed quietly and smiled.

'That's fine, Hu. This can be our little secret. Our little secret.' Then he laughed again.

'OK,' he said. 'Let's do something on tenses. Things you usually do in the past. Page 14, exercise 3a.' Mr Stanyer handed Hu an old copy of the students' workbook that went with their textbook.

Then he settled down with a magazine. Hu couldn't see the magazine, but Mr Stanyer gave it all his attention, smiling and laughing as he turned the pages. He seemed not to know Hu was in the classroom.

Hu worked through the exercises. At first they seemed easy. But then she wanted to ask a question.

'Mr Stanyer?'

'Mmm.' His eyes didn't leave the magazine.

'Is "used to" a tense?'

'Is "used to" a tense?' Mr Stanyer mocked Hu's voice. 'The answers are at the back of the book, Hu.'

'Yes, and I've got the answers right. *All* right. But it doesn't seem like a tense. It doesn't change and ...'

'So you want to be the expert now?' Mr Stanyer looked in the drawer in his desk. He pulled out a grammar book and threw it on the desk in front of Hu.

'Yeah, it's a kind of tense, er, in the past. Look it up.' He pushed his chair back and slowly stood up. 'Listen, I've got to make a phone call ... I'm going to the teachers' room. I'll be back in five minutes, maybe ten.' He carefully put the magazine back in the drawer, locked the desk and left the room.

He didn't go to the teachers' room. Hu saw him walking through the school gate and across the road to the Chinese shop.

Hu looked up 'used to' in the grammar book. The explanation didn't help her. She started the next exercise.

It was nearly half past four when Mr Stanyer came back. His face was red and he smelled more strongly of cigarettes, and, she guessed, rice whisky.

'Any problems?'

'No, I got all the answers right. But I still don't understand if "used to" is a tense or . . .'

'Let's just call it an expression. Listen, honey, sometimes we just say things a certain way in English.' Mr Stanyer yawned. Hu said nothing.

'OK, we've done enough for today,' said Mr Stanyer.

'We?' thought Hu.

'So . . . er, that's five hundred Baht. That's what we agreed?'

Hu didn't argue. That's what Mr Stanyer had agreed, with himself. With all the pocket money she had saved and her lunch money for the last two days, Hu had exactly five hundred Baht.

'See you on Wednesday,' said Mr Stanyer, counting the hundred Baht notes and smiling to himself.

But how would she find the money for Wednesday? How would she stand six more weeks with Mr Declan Stanyer?

Chapter 7   Of rings and lies

The two policemen entered the classroom during her English lesson. One was fat, his stomach tight in his brown uniform, the other was small and thin. They had guns.

'We have come for Hu Jian Ming. She must come now. She stole a gold ring.'

Before Hu could say anything, the small policeman roughly took her by the arm and pulled her towards the classroom door. Marwa started crying.

'Huuuu . . .'

Hu started to try and speak. 'You must tell my father . . .' But the words wouldn't come out. She couldn't breathe. What was happening? Mr Stanyer started laughing. The other children started laughing. The thin policeman was pulling her through the classroom door. Marwa was screaming. Hu couldn't breathe. 'You must tell my father . . .'

*   *   *

She was awake, breathing heavily, her heart beating fast. It was quite dark. Bangkok was very strange at four o'clock in the morning because it was so quiet. From time to time there was the noise of a motorbike, but even the building work had stopped until first light. Where was she?

'I am in my own bed. I am at home. There are no policemen. I did not steal the ring.' Hu tried to calm herself. Slowly her breathing and her heart returned to normal. It was a dream.

Of course! The ring! Aunty Wang's ring. Aunty Wang was Hu's mother's cousin. The ring had belonged to Aunty Wang's mother before she died. When Aunty Wang went to live in America with her new husband, she had given the ring to Hu.

'My husband is a rich man. I will have all the rings and all the gold I want,' she had told Hu.

The ring was very old and very valuable. Hu kept it in a jewellery box her mother had given her on her sixteenth birthday.

'I can sell it,' Hu told herself. 'Later I can work and buy another one just like it. It will just be like borrowing the money.'

Hu decided she would carefully write down the dates and the amounts she paid to Mr Stanyer after each 'lesson'. She would only spend what she needed to. She felt very bad about the idea, but she couldn't see any other way out of her situation. It was a long time before she slept again.

* * *

It was Saturday. Hu had told her mother she was going to the Dusit zoo with Marwa and Yoshiko. Hu's father was playing golf with his important visitor that day. Her mother was finishing a dress for the English woman in the apartment above theirs. Hu was alone in the apartment. She made herself a snack to eat and then started across Bangkok.

It is always easy to find a jewellery shop in Bangkok, but Hu didn't want to be recognised, so she travelled to the other side of the city. The bus journey was long and hot and uncomfortable – even on a Saturday, the traffic was very bad. But she had a seat, and she sat holding tight to the gold ring in its box, with a mixture of fear and guilt.

She tried three jewellery shops before she could get a good price. In the third shop there was an old Chinese man with two gold teeth. Hu could argue better in her own language. The man didn't seem to believe that the ring belonged to Hu, but she managed to raise the price. Finally the man said that she was robbing a poor old man and disappeared into the back of the dark shop. He came back with lots of five hundred Baht notes. He counted out the sum they had agreed and gave the notes to Hu. Now she felt like a thief.

Hu buried the notes right at the bottom of her shoulder bag and walked out into the sunshine.

Hu couldn't go home so soon. She sat at a tiny table on the pavement and ordered a bowl of noodles. They were hot and delicious. But she couldn't eat them. She thought of the money in the bag at her feet and felt sick with fear. Bangkok is a safe enough city if you are careful, but Hu had never had so much money before. And it didn't feel like her own money.

After a while it was time to go home. She would tell her mother she didn't feel well and had to come back from the zoo early.

Another lie, but now she had the money for her lessons.

Chapter 8　*A proud father*

The next few weeks were a little easier. Hu couldn't stop feeling guilty about selling her gold ring, and worried about the money hidden in her jewellery box. She still slept badly. She spent as little of the money as she could and wrote down each amount she 'borrowed'. Hu tried to keep the lessons secret, but her friends soon learnt about her situation. They were very good to her.

Lessons! They were not real lessons. Hu learnt to do the simple exercises Mr Stanyer gave her from the workbook at the beginning of the lesson, and then when he went to 'make a telephone call', she would do her other homework. She didn't ask questions. 'That's just how we say things in English,' Mr Stanyer would say. How she hated that!

And how she hated him, his smell of sweat and cigarettes, his laziness. She hated the way he laughed at his magazines, how he sat with his feet on the desk. But he was too stupid to worry about. And now that she was paying for lessons, he was giving her higher marks.

One day he looked up from his magazine and found Hu yawning and stretching. She was bored, and she had not slept well.

'You uncomfortable?' he said. 'These classroom chairs are uncomfortable. And it's kind of hot in here.' As usual, there were dark marks under the arms of his shirt. Mr Stanyer pushed his hands across his bald head. He took a deep breath, smiled, and then said:

'Hu, we don't have to be uncomfortable. We don't have to have these lessons here. You could come back to my place in Soi 35. You could relax there ... be more comfortable.'

'No!' said Hu, looking Mr Stanyer directly in the eye. She said no with such strength, with so much anger, Mr Stanyer looked as if she had hit him.

Then he went to make a telephone call. He never mentioned the idea again.

*   *   *

Hu learnt much more English in the library with John than with Mr Stanyer. John told her about his home in America, about his friends and his family. Hu told him about China, about the many changes in her life and the lives of her friends and family. They talked about Thailand, and of their hopes for their future lives. John wanted to be an engineer; Hu was not sure if she wanted to be a doctor or a singer.

The school show was the best, the most exciting part of her life at school. She knew her father would not be happy about her taking part in the show. 'Your studies must come first. You won't become a doctor by singing in shows,' he would say. But when she told her mother, her mother was delighted and helped her learn the songs. When she was not doing one of her little jobs, baby-sitting or making clothes, Hu's mother came to watch them practising. She found the music and the style of singing very different from her own training, but it made her happy and excited. Afterwards, Hu would hear her mother singing as she prepared their supper. Sometimes Hu's mother would sing her favourite love songs from Anhui opera, and sometimes she would try the songs from 'The Wizard of Oz' in her strange Chinese English. It made Hu laugh.

As she had expected, Hu's father was not very happy about the school show, but he was glad to see Hu's mother enjoying herself. He pointed out that Hu needed all her spare time for studying, but left the decision to her. After a while he said nothing. Perhaps he was too busy and too tired to argue.

All the talk among her friends was about the field trip to Khao Yai. They talked about which groups they would join and which activities they would do together. Hu didn't like to feel jealous. She had told Mr Rodriguez she couldn't go because she had to prepare for the Chinese New Year holiday. Mr Rodriguez was disappointed. Hu was his star pupil in biology. Hu said nothing when her friends were making their plans. She told herself it was more important to prepare for the selection tests for the IB. The tests were a week after the field trip.

*   *   *

One morning, a week before the field trip, Hu was woken up by the sound of her father coughing. He was on the balcony outside her room, watering mother's 'little jungle'. A few seconds later he knocked on her bedroom door.

'Jian Ming, I want to talk to you.'

It sounded important. Hu put on her dressing gown over her pyjamas and joined her father at the breakfast table. Her mother was in the kitchen.

'Father, you're smoking! It's not even seven o'clock!' said Hu.

'Oh. Sorry.' He put out his cigarette. 'Important meeting today. Sorry.' He held up some papers.

'What's this?'

Hu could see that it was the information about the Khao Yai field trip.

'Your mother was looking in your school bag for your dirty sports shirt,' he added.

'I'm sorry, father.'

'And she found this. Why didn't you tell us about this?' Hu's father looked disappointed.

'I'm sorry. I . . . I forgot. It's not important. I don't want to go.' Hu couldn't look at her father.

He lit another cigarette without thinking. Hu said nothing. Her father smoked the cigarette and then asked her:

'Which is it? You forgot? You thought it wasn't important? Or you don't want to go?'

'But father, it's so expensive . . .'

'But Jian Ming, it's so important. It's biology. If you want to be a doctor, you must be good at biology. There is always money for your education. And I know how much you love plants and birds and animals. You need a break from Bangkok.' He sighed. 'I know I'm always too busy to give us a holiday, I'm sorry. My work is so important.'

'It's too late now. I've told them I cannot go.'

'You told them you had to prepare for the Chinese New Year holiday. You know that's not true.' Her father looked hurt.

'You've spoken to Mr Rodriguez?' asked Hu.

'I have. And it's not too late. Another student had to drop out. He has to go into hospital for a small operation.'

Hu's father stood up, checking his jacket pockets for cigarettes.

'It's all arranged. All paid for. You silly girl.' He laughed and started coughing. As he got to the door of the apartment he shouted goodbye to Hu and her mother, and then left.

Hu didn't know if she should cry or shout for joy. Khao Yai National Park! Next week!

Chapter 9   *Losing the right path*

Hu sat with her feet in the water. It was hot, but she didn't feel too hot with her feet in the water. The others were on the other side of the pool formed by the waterfall. They were feeding the last of the bread to some grey fish. What were these fish? Hu wondered. They could ask Mr Rodriguez when they returned to the Field Centre.

It was a moment to herself. It was the first moment to herself for three days, since she left Bangkok.

Hu sat on the warm rock and put her head back. She looked up through the trees, up and up until maybe a hundred metres above her she could see bright blue sky among the leaves and branches. Around her she could hear water crashing into the pool and her friends laughing as the fish fought and jumped for pieces of bread. From the trees came the sound of birdsong, and always, never stopping, the continuous noise of unseen insects. Up here, about one thousand metres above sea level in the Dongrak mountains, the air was clean and smelled of plants and flowers; Hu could taste its freshness.

Her new happiness had been growing since she left Bangkok. As they had passed Don Muang International Airport and the last of the traffic jams, Hu had turned in her seat at the back of the tour bus and looked back. She could see the milky orange cloud of dirt hanging above the tall buildings of the great city. She could still see the cloud fifty, even eighty kilometres away.

The Thai students had started singing just beyond the airport. They sang one of Hu's favourite pop songs, 'Mae Ben Rae', which means 'never mind'. It was perfect for her mood. *Mae Ben Rae*, never mind money, never mind Mr Stanyer, the IB tests.

As the Thai students sang, the other students had joined in. Soon the students in the school show were singing some of the songs from 'The Wizard of Oz'. Hu was asked to sing some of the show's big hit songs and Hu gave her very best performance. They had sung all the way to the national park's Field Centre where they were staying.

Over the next two days Hu had had very little time to herself. Mr Rodriguez kept them busy all day collecting, drawing maps, looking at different plants and animals and trying to name them. After supper, the teachers gave them lectures on the park. The days were long and tiring, and Hu slept better than she had for weeks.

Now Hu could hear that Sean Payne had joined their group by the waterfall. It seemed that every time Hu looked round he was next to her. He was too friendly. He wanted to give her things, a cola, chewing gum, even a cigarette. (He was always smoking when the teachers were not looking.) Marwa and Yoshiko were very good. They knew she didn't want to be alone with Sean and stayed close to her when Sean tried to talk to her. She didn't want to be unkind, but she wanted some time to herself. Or she wanted time to talk to Marwa or John by herself. But Sean was always there.

Hu closed her eyes and listened to the music of the waterfall, and smelled the perfume of the air. But where was Sean now?

Suddenly there was a scream. It was Sean's voice. Hu opened her eyes and for a moment was blind in the brilliant sunshine. 'Stupid!' she said to herself. Another scream, Sean's, came from the trees behind her.

'Help! Please help me! I've broken my leg!' Sean was screaming in English and Thai.

'Sean's in trouble,' said John. 'We've got to do something!'

'He probably just wants us to go and look for him,' said Hu.

Another scream.

'Over there,' said Thomas, pointing to the trees behind Hu. 'We must go and look. We must stay together.'

'He's probably just being silly,' said Hu, putting on her walking boots.

Another scream. Thomas ran towards the noise. The others followed him. When they left the path, walking was difficult. Sean was somewhere up ahead. Then the noise stopped. It was cool by the waterfall, but as soon as they started into the trees it was hot. The plants scratched them and Yoshiko was frightened of snakes. They came to an open space among the trees, and stopped to wait for Marwa.

'He's stopped screaming. We must find him!' said Thomas.

'He was here. I can smell cigarettes,' Hu said.

'He's just playing games with us,' said Yoshiko.

There was a louder scream. 'Help me! I'm dying!' The screaming seemed very close.

'This way!' shouted Thomas, and he started back into the trees. The others followed. They crossed a stream.

Marwa found it difficult, but John helped her. They heard Sean calling close by.

They came to another space. Sean was not there. His calls had stopped for a moment.

'This is stupid,' said Hu. 'It's just a game for him.'

'I guess . . .' John began.

'Snake!' screamed Sean.

Thomas was running. The others followed.

The search continued for almost an hour. They crossed streams, climbed higher and higher.

'Stop!' said Hu. 'This is stupid. Look!' She bent down and picked up an empty cigarette packet. 'This is just a stupid game.'

They waited a few moments. John passed round his water bottle. Nobody spoke.

'Roaaaarrrgh!' A horrible noise came from behind them. 'Don't you know they have tigers here?' said Sean, standing up from behind a bush. He had a can of cola in one hand and a cigarette in the other.

Sean had not broken his leg. He was smiling. A moment passed. Thomas spoke first.

'You're an idiot!'

Sean said nothing. Then John spoke.

'I think we're lost!'

Chapter 10　*Towards the truth*

They looked at each other in silence. Quietly Marwa began to cry. Sean looked as if he was going to say something, but Thomas gave him such an angry look he changed his mind. Sean began to look in his bag for something.

'What are we going to do?' asked Yoshiko. She had her arm round Marwa to comfort her.

'We must think,' said Thomas.

'I can phone,' said Sean holding up his mobile phone.

'Yes, but first we have to have some idea where we are,' said John. 'We need something we can tell them to look for.'

'We can only be about an hour's walk from the waterfall,' said Thomas.

'But which direction?' asked Hu. 'We changed direction so many times.'

'Sorry,' said Sean. Nobody said anything.

'We could climb to the top of the mountain and look around?' offered Yoshiko after a minute.

'No. You would just see trees. The answer must be down, not up. We have been going up all day, following the waterfalls. The last one is at nine hundred and seventy metres, and we're higher than that,' said John. 'We'll find the road again if we travel downwards.'

'Yeah, you're right,' said Thomas. 'And the main road through the park is west of the waterfalls. The Pak Chong to Prachinburi road more or less cuts the park in half from north to south. We're in the eastern half. So we must walk west and downwards.'

'Don't worry, Marwa,' said Hu. 'We'll find the path.'

'No!' said Thomas. Sean had a can of cola in his hand, ready to open it. 'No! Sean, we must save water.'

'This is cola, Thomas . . .' said Sean with a silly smile.

'Don't drink it now, stupid!' shouted Thomas.

'OK,' said Sean. He put the can back in his bag.

'West is this way, I think,' said Hu. She was pointing at a thick wall of trees. 'We might have to go round those trees.'

'Follow me!' said Thomas. 'John, you must stay at the back with Marwa. And Sean, you mustn't play any more stupid games.' They set out behind Thomas. Sean pretended to walk like a soldier, quietly saying, 'must, mustn't, must, mustn't' with each step.

* * *

It is impossible to walk in a straight line in thickly forested hill country. Progress was slow and painful. They often had to stop and sometimes the boys would argue about which way was west. Sean and Thomas argued more and more through the afternoon, and Marwa looked very tired and frightened.

They stopped by a stream. The boys were washing the dirt and blood from their arms while the girls tried to decide which way to try next.

Hu looked at Sean. 'Do you want to make that phone call now, Sean?'

None of them knew the phone number of the Field Centre.

'I'll phone my mother at work,' suggested Sean. Thomas raised his eyebrows and was about to say something, but Hu was standing next to him and stepped hard on his foot. Thomas said nothing.

They waited in total silence as Sean rang. They all felt happy when someone answered it. Sean turned his back to them while he talked very quickly in Thai. Then he started shaking the phone. He tried to phone again. They were all looking at him.

'I think the phone is dead. I was talking to my mother last night for maybe half an hour.'

'Did you tell your mother what's happened?' asked John.

'Yeah,' said Sean sadly. 'But I don't think she believed me. I think she thought I was making up stories . . .'

Thomas said something in German. To his surprise, Sean said something back at him in German. For a moment Thomas didn't know what to say.

'You guys!' shouted John. 'That's enough! We've got to think about stopping. We won't get any further today.'

'Yes!' said Thomas. 'First we must find a place. Then we must share some food and water. We must make a fire.'

'Must, must, always must! Who makes you the boss? Just because your father's a policeman,' shouted Sean.

Thomas was much shorter than Sean, but that didn't stop him. He threw himself at Sean.

Sean easily held him off. Thomas was kicking and shouting in German.

'My father is Chief Police Officer at the German Embassy,' shouted Thomas breathing heavily. 'At least he's not a barman. And he didn't marry a "dancer" from a bar!'

Sean's face went white. He held Thomas very tightly by the arms, and lifted him off the ground.

'Listen, Kuhlauf,' said Sean in a low, angry voice. 'My father owns a chain of restaurants in Bangkok, Hua Hin and Rayong.' Sean was breathing very heavily. Thomas was suddenly very frightened. 'My mother owned and managed one of the restaurants when my father bought it. Now she's company accountant.'

Sean put his face very close to Thomas' face and said slowly and angrily, 'Don't you ever repeat that rubbish again!'

There was a moment of total silence. Suddenly he dropped Thomas. John quickly held Thomas from behind. Sean and Thomas were both breathing heavily, staring at each other angrily.

* * *

Hu, Marwa and Yoshiko took charge. They decided to stay where they were, close to water to wash in and with a few metres space before the trees closed in. They went to look for wood, Thomas and John in one direction, Hu and Sean in the other direction. Yoshiko stayed with Marwa who was very tired and frightened. The two of them tried to clear some space to sit and sleep in.

Men always like making a fire. The three boys worked hard collecting wood and leaves. They carefully built the fire and Sean encouraged a small flame from his cigarette lighter to catch the dry leaves. As darkness closed in they started sharing out what little food they had. It was clear that Sean and Thomas had cooled their anger. John tried to persuade Thomas to apologise to Sean, but Thomas was too angry or embarrassed. But they did sit and share a few biscuits and sweets peacefully.

Hu found Sean sitting next to her. John was sitting next to Thomas, as far away from Sean as possible, and Marwa was asleep with her head on Hu's knee. Sean started chatting to Yoshiko in Japanese.

'How many languages do you speak, Sean?' asked Hu.

'English from my father, Thai from my mother,' then in Chinese he said, 'I learnt Chinese from my mother's mother. I also know some Japanese and German from the tourists when I help in one of my father's restaurants in the school holidays. I like languages.'

Yoshiko and Hu were surprised. Hu said so in Chinese and Yoshiko in Japanese. Sean smiled a kind smile.

'Maybe I'm not as stupid as I look.' He was looking at Hu. She could see his eyes shining in the light of the fire. 'Maybe you shouldn't listen to what people say about me. I don't believe what they are saying about you, Hu.'

Hu sat up quickly. 'And what are they saying about me?' she said angrily.

'That you're one of Mr Stanyer's little friends.'

Hu was silent a moment. Sean Payne! He always said the most stupid things. She almost shouted, 'Who says? Who says that?'

'Sorry, Hu, it's true. People are saying it. Don't be angry. It's rubbish,' said Yoshiko.

Hu was frightened, angry. '*They* say??'

'Mostly your understudy, Melanie Gibson, the singing

53

duck. You should be careful of her, Hu. She has a nasty way of talking about people.'

*   *   *

'Just you wait! You'll see! I'll get you!' Hu could hear Melanie's words ringing in her head. Hu tried to sleep, but she was thinking, thinking all the time. Marwa's head was heavy on her knees. Hu couldn't feel her legs.

How long before her parents might hear something about Mr Stanyer and the English lessons? Hu looked into the dark. How long?

Chapter 11 *A way out?*

'Hu?'

Hu could feel him looking at her. It was still dark. Her leg hurt and she wanted to move Marwa, who was still sleeping. It was cold too. Hu was hungry. The fire was finished.

'Shhhh!' said Hu, quietly. 'Don't wake Marwa, Sean.'

'OK.' Sean's voice was quiet. He spoke softly in Chinese.

'I just wanted to explain. I don't believe this stuff about Declan Stanyer. I know his game.' Sean sat closer to her.

'Noroko Ito. Ilse Sphenson. Fatima Rashid. Darunee Phalavadhana. It's a long list. He's been doing this since he came to the school.'

'Doing what?' asked Hu.

'His game. Girls. His "private lesson" game. Rich girls. Pretty girls.'

'I'm not rich, Sean,' said Hu. She could sense him smiling.

'Maybe not. But he thinks you are. First you get the bad results, then he says you need extra private lessons. You don't tell your parents, do you?'

'No. But Sean, how do you know?'

'He tried it with my sister. She told me, and I, er, spoke to him. He didn't like that one little bit.' Sean paused. 'Did he invite you back to his apartment to be "more comfortable"? No?'

'Yes, he did. I said no,' said Hu. 'He does this to other students?'

Sean nodded.

Hu thought for a moment.

'Sean, what can I do?'

There was a moment's silence.

'I don't know, Hu. Do you want me to speak to him? That man is bad news.' Sean sounded sad.

'And now Melanie Gibson is saying things about me?' Hu listened to the music of the stream close by.

Perhaps Sean nodded. It was too dark to see.

'Sean. Listen . . .'

They listened. They listened to the music of the stream.

'Which way does water go?' asked Hu.

'Hmm. Down. That's called "gravity",' said Sean.

'Down means out, don't you see? We're sitting in the Dongrak mountains. *Out* is the Korat plateau.'

'I get you,' said Sean. He sounded excited.

'So we follow the stream, the water . . . we follow it *out* of the park. No more turning in circles, no more arguments about which way is west.'

Sean sighed. 'So *down* means *out*. Cool, Hu! We just follow the water.' Sean smiled in the dark.

Now there was some hope.

* * *

Dawn in a tropical forest is not a peaceful matter. Everything that walks, or flies, or moves, wakes up screaming 'hungry!' It is like a crazy symphony orchestra tuning up before a concert. It is a market place, a building site, an animal city, busy, busy, busy. The rush hour.

'Wake up, Hu. Breakfast!' shouted Marwa. Marwa was still very hungry, but she was no longer the tired and frightened child of yesterday. Hu had been asleep for perhaps an hour. Marwa and Yoshiko pulled her to her feet. Marwa gave Hu some sweets and her last biscuit.

'Hi!' shouted Sean, climbing back from the stream. 'Your turn!' He and John and Thomas had washed first. Now it was the girls' turn.

Ten minutes later they all met at the spot where the fire had been the night before. Sean tried to use his mobile phone again, but it still didn't work.

'Sean told me about your idea, Hu. It's the only idea we have. We'll follow the direction of the water – the stream – down and, I hope, out of here,' said Thomas.

'I'll go first with John. Sean will stay with Marwa at the back,' said Thomas.

'I'm OK now!' shouted Marwa.

'Don't worry, little lady. We'll be out of here soon,' said Sean. 'And I'll be right behind you.'

They began to move slowly down the stream.

* * *

It wasn't easy. True, they were going downwards. But, as they did so, the stream became wider and steeper. They climbed from rock to rock. Marwa seemed much stronger today, and Thomas seemed ready to hurry, to take chances. They had water from the stream, which they didn't want to drink, and nothing left to eat. They all knew that if they didn't find the path today there would be nothing for them tonight. Thomas raced ahead, and Sean was very kind to Marwa, pulling her, sometimes half carrying her from rock to rock as they climbed down the stream.

Towards the middle of the morning they heard a helicopter. Sean stopped in the middle of the stream and spread his arms.

'Mama . . . I love you!' he called.

'We must make a sign. Make smoke! A fire!' screamed Thomas from below.

Sean climbed out of the water and collected some dry wood. Hu helped him. Sean tried to start a fire, but his cigarette lighter was wet. When the leaves and wood finally caught fire, the helicopter had gone.

Thomas said something in German. Then he ran back to the stream.

'Come on!' he shouted, running through the moving water of the stream. He was soon out of sight.

Thomas screamed. There was a crash and the sound of water.

John and Sean ran to the stream first. There were two large rocks and then a drop of about five metres, a small waterfall. In the pool below they could see Thomas lying in the water. He wasn't moving. The water next to his head on the right side was red.

Sean didn't wait, not for a moment. He threw his bag onto the bank of the stream and dived into the pool beside Thomas's body. The others climbed down the bank to join him.

They found Sean holding Thomas in his arms by the side of the pool.

'He's OK,' said Sean. 'He's breathing. But he's unconscious. He hit his head.'

'How did you know the water was deep enough, Sean?' asked Yoshiko.

'I didn't,' said Sean.

There was a deep cut on Thomas's head. He seemed to be asleep.

'John, you take my bag. I'll take Thomas.' Sean lifted Thomas onto his shoulders. Thomas seemed to weigh nothing.

*   *   *

Sean carried Thomas for another two hours before they found a road. It was made of earth, but wide enough for a car. They stopped. Sean gently put Thomas down in the grass beside the track. The others sat or lay by the road. They were exhausted. Soon they heard the sound of an engine. A lorry stopped about a hundred metres in front of them. Hu stood up and started to wave.

A tiny man in a grey uniform jumped down from the lorry. He pulled out a gun and pointed it in the air, shooting the gun and screaming and laughing.

'What's he saying?' asked Marwa.

'He says we are the BIA students that got lost,' said Sean. 'He says it's OK! There are helicopters. Television. Television? This guy is crazy,' Sean was laughing. The little man climbed back into his lorry and drove close to them.

'He says to climb in,' said Sean.

*   *   *

Hu sat in the back of the oil company car. She was half asleep. Her father sat next to her.

'Hu, I'm so glad you're safe. When your friend Sean

59

made that telephone call, it was on the Channel 7 television news. We've been so worried.' The car moved quickly along the highway back to Bangkok.

'Please don't worry, father,' said Hu, sleepily.

'You're safe now. We'll soon be home. Oh, and Hu?' Hu's father said softly.

'Hmm ... ?' said Hu. She was falling asleep.

'One piece of good news. Your Aunty Wang the one who gave you the ring? She's coming to stay with us.'

But Hu was already asleep.

Chapter 12 *Nothing but the truth*

Hu and John met in the library after lunch. Hu couldn't help crying.

'But Hu, I knew Stanyer was asking a lot for his private lessons. But you sold your Aunty's ring!'

'It was my ring!' cried Hu. 'But I didn't know what to do.'

Miss Paula looked over her glasses and coughed quietly. She was very worried about Hu. Since she had come back from the field trip she had seemed unhappy.

'When does your aunt come, Hu?' asked John.

'Sunday. And Stanyer wants two more lessons before the English test for the IB on Friday.' Hu tried to stop crying.

'And from what Sean says, it's what he always does. Did you speak to the other girls he talked about?'

'I feel too stupid. I don't know what to say?'

'But Hu, what about Darunee Phalavadhana? Her father's Wiwat Phalavadhana. He's an important official in the Ministry of the Interior. If he finds out ... My mother knows him. Perhaps I could speak to her?' John offered.

'But what can you say? "Are you one of Stanyer's little friends?" Like Melanie is saying about me?'

'I don't know, Hu. I think you've got to tell someone about it. The story is coming out already. You need to tell your side of the story.'

Hu covered her face with her hands and cried. 'But I can't! Who can I tell?'

'My mother?' suggested John. 'She knows you from the school show ... and she likes you. She knows there's nothing wrong with your English.'

'No!' Hu had raised her voice. Miss Paula looked across at them. 'I'm sorry, John, I need to be on my own.' She got up quickly. 'I need to go and wash my face.'

John stayed in the library for a few minutes after Hu had left. He tried to think. Eventually, he made a decision. He decided to tell his mother, even if Hu wouldn't like it. He felt sad because he didn't want to do anything behind Hu's back, but he couldn't see any other way to help her.

Mr Riding, the school counsellor, spoke to Hu as she hurried across the school yard from the library. He fixed Hu with his hard blue eyes and smiled.

'What's the hurry, Hu?' His stare seemed to look right into her mind. 'You've been crying.'

Hu nodded silently. Mr Riding frightened her. People said he could have power over you with his eyes. His job was to counsel students with 'problems', but he seemed to find problems when people didn't even know they had them.

'I've been watching you recently. You seem worried and unhappy a lot of the time, and I've seen you crying several times. I think we need to talk. Come to my office.'

'But Mr Riding, I have classes ...'

Mr Riding stared at her hard. Then he turned and walked to his office. Hu followed, her head down to hide the tears.

From the library window John saw Mr Riding and Hu entering Mr Riding's counselling office. He picked up his books and half ran to his mother's office.

* * *

'Sit down, Hu, and try and relax,' said Mr Riding.

'Relax?' thought Hu. 'Does he think I'm stupid?' She sat very straight on the edge of a low armchair. Mr Riding went to the window, turned and looked down at Hu. He was a tall man in his fifties with red hair which was turning white.

'Do you mind if I smoke?' he asked.

Hu did mind if he smoked, and it was against school rules. Mr Riding got out his pipe and started to light it.

'No, go ahead,' said Hu.

'Like I said, I've been very worried about you for some time. Some of the other teachers have said that you're unhappy. How are things at home?'

'Fine,' said Hu quietly.

'You get on with your parents? I mean, you talk about things with them?'

'Yes.' Mr Riding waited, staring at her. Hu felt uncomfortable. 'I ... I do housework with my mother and she helps me with my singing ...'

'But can you talk about serious things with her?'

Hu said nothing.

'What about your father?'

'He's always very busy. We talk sometimes in the mornings.'

'Do you talk about important things, Hu?' Mr Riding left the window and sat down heavily in front of her. 'I mean, you're growing up, Hu?' he said very quietly, never letting his hard blue eyes leave hers.

Hu held her hands very tightly together and looked away.

'I understand you've been seeing a lot of Mr Stanyer recently.'

'He's been giving me extra classes,' said Hu.

'Look at me, Hu.' Hu tried. 'Do you like Mr Stanyer?'

'No!' shouted Hu, looking straight at Mr Riding.

'Relax!' said Mr Riding, with a false laugh. He paused. 'It's not so unusual for a young woman of your age to be ... to be attracted to an older man, a man in an ... an important position.' Mr Riding smiled to himself.

Hu couldn't breathe, she was so angry. She decided not to speak.

'Uh huh,' said Mr Riding, standing up again and walking towards the window. 'Does your father know about these, er, "extra lessons", Hu?'

'No. I ...'

'Hu,' said Mr Riding, 'are you scared of your father? Does he shout at you? Has he ever hit you?'

That was when Hu could no longer keep her anger inside. Suddenly she started crying, and could not stop. Somehow she told Mr Riding the whole story.

At the end of the interview, Mr Riding put his arm round her and led her to the door.

'What you've said is very serious. These are very serious things to say about a teacher.' Hu tried to move away from him.

'But ...'

'And I'm not sure you completely understand your own feelings about this man, Hu.' He smiled. 'But don't worry. I think I can sort this out. But we'll need to talk about this again. In the meantime, I shall have to discuss this with my colleagues.'

Hu felt her stomach turn to ice.

'Now, off you go back to class, Hu. And try not to worry.'

Hu didn't go back to class. She went to the main office and told the school nurse she was feeling ill and then walked towards the school gate. She met Mrs Patel carrying a pile of music.

'Are you going home, Hu?' asked Mrs Patel. 'What about the show? We have a rehearsal after school. Are you OK?'

'I'm sorry, Mrs Patel, I . . .' Hu started crying again.

'It is all right now, my dear, Melanie can take your place. She took your place when you were in Khao Yai. She is getting much better. But you must not miss any more, or I'll have to let her take the part of Dorothy in the show.'

Hu ran. She ran home, blinded by tears. She let herself into the empty apartment, locked herself in her room and threw herself upon her bed, crying.

* * *

Mrs Truman, John's mother, was late home. She had been looking at Mr Stanyer's test records in the main school office and making telephone calls. She said nothing to John and Mary when she entered her apartment, but went straight into her study and closed the door. She picked up the telephone.

'Can I speak to Wiwat Phalavadhana ... Wiwat? Is that you?'

The telephones were busy in Bangkok that night.

*   *   *

It was the telephone ringing which woke Hu a little later. She had cried herself to sleep.

'Hello?' she said, her voice dry with crying.

'May I speak with Mr Hu An Yuan? It's Mr David Riding here from the Bangkok International Academy.'

Hu's heart stopped. 'It's Hu here. Father is still at work. Do you have his number?'

'And your mother's not there? OK. I'll phone him at work.' He paused. 'Hu, are you still there?'

Hu was thinking, 'What can I do?'

'Hu, I should tell you there will be a meeting tomorrow at twelve o'clock. The things you told me about Mr Stanyer are very serious. You can't just say those things about a teacher.'

'But, Mr Riding, you were counselling me. I trusted you!' cried Hu.

'My main responsibility is to the school,' said Mr Riding. 'Just make sure you and your father come to the meeting. Twelve o'clock.'

Hu made herself a cup of tea. She was too tired to cry any more. What could she do?

The phone rang again. It was John.

'Sorry, Hu, I wanted to phone you earlier, but my mother's been using the phone for hours. Are you OK? You weren't in class this afternoon, and I saw you with Mr Riding. What does he want?'

66

Hu quickly explained about the meeting tomorrow. What could she do?

John's answer was simple. 'Tell your parents the truth. Tell them everything. Tell them the truth, the whole truth, and nothing but the truth. That's all you can do.'

That was all she could do. Nothing but the truth. Hu decided she would tell the truth. The truth, the whole truth, and nothing but the truth.

She could hear her father and mother's voices on the landing outside the apartment and a key in the lock of the entrance door.

The truth, the whole truth, and nothing but the truth.

*   *   *

Later that night, much later, Verity Truman drove back to the school. She went to the main office and took the master keys to the classrooms. Quietly she let herself into Mr Stanyer's classroom and tried the drawer of his desk. Locked, as she expected.

'God forgive me!' she said under her breath. She took a knife from her pocket and opened the locked drawer.

Chapter 13 *The moment of truth*

In an office in the Upper School building, Verity Truman was sitting, staring at her telephone.

'Come on, Wiwat. Come on!' She looked at her watch again. Nearly twelve o'clock.

* * *

Meanwhile, in another part of the school, Hu and her mother and father were waiting outside the principal's office. They could hear voices from inside. Hu and her mother and father said nothing.

Hu thought about her parents. They had been surprisingly calm when she had told them her story. Her mother had been unhappy about Aunty Wang's ring. 'It's been in the family for a long time!' she had said. 'Your Aunty Wang had it, *her* mother, and now you!'

But her father didn't think it was so very important. 'Aunty Wang had so many jewels, she won't notice,' he had said. Then, very sadly, he added, 'Hu, it was your ring, and your decision. You are almost an adult, a young adult. Now this is your problem, your responsibility. It was yours to sell. But you should not have sold it secretly.'

Hu's father had seemed sad, not angry, Very carefully, he had questioned Hu for every detail of her problems with Mr Stanyer. Like a good lawyer, he had got the whole story from her – he had even made her show him the book where she had written down the dates of the classes and the money she had paid Mr Stanyer.

'But why didn't you tell me?' he had asked.

'Because you want me to be a doctor so much, and with bad results in English, they won't let me do the IB. I didn't want to disappoint you, father.'

It was late when Hu's father was satisfied that he had the whole story. He told Hu to go to bed, but before she left she asked him.

'Father, do you believe me?'

Hu's father didn't answer immediately.

'I want to believe you,' he said at last. 'You wanted to improve your results, so you did extra lessons. That is not a bad thing, although you should have told us. But these are terrible things you say about Mr Stanyer. I want to believe you, but there have been too many lies, and too many secrets. And I haven't met Mr Stanyer yet. I want to believe you, but I must decide tomorrow in the meeting. Now, good night, little one.'

*   *   *

Mr Grisman stood very tall and serious in his black suit and Cambridge University tie. He stood at the door of his office and asked Hu and her parents to come in.

'Do sit down. Let me introduce you,' Mr Grisman said.

Sitting at the long table in Mr Grisman's very grand office were three other men in suits. By the door Mr Stanyer sat, staring at nothing.

Hu and her mother and father sat down at the table. Mr Grisman took his seat opposite Mr Stanyer and the Hu family. On his left Mr Riding sat, leaning back and playing with his empty pipe. On his right was Khun Preecha, chair of the Board of Governors. He was a tall Thai man with grey hair and he looked at Hu steadily with sad, intelligent eyes. He didn't smile.

Mr Grisman continued in his important voice.

'This is a very serious matter, very serious indeed. Your daughter has said some very serious things about our Mr Stanyer. Your daughter's behaviour is quite unacceptable. She has deliberately tried to harm him,' Mr Grisman raised his voice, 'and the good name of the Academy itself.' He paused. Khun Preecha looked embarrassed.

Hu looked at her mother and father. Her mother looked pale and frightened. Her father's face showed no emotion at all. He simply sat and stared at Mr Grisman without expression.

Mr Grisman continued. 'I have invited Khun Preecha to be here because we must decide if, because of the things she's said about Mr Stanyer, Hu can continue to study at the Academy.'

Hu's father said nothing, and the expression on his face didn't change. Hu's mother was looking down, afraid to meet Mr Grisman's eyes. Mr Stanyer was trying not to smile. Hu closed her eyes.

*   *   *

In her office, Verity Truman was walking up and down. She picked up the telephone to see if it was working and quickly put it down again. 'Wiwat, where are you? They must have started by now!' she said to herself.

*   *   *

'Now,' said Mr Grisman, 'we must consider just exactly what Hu Jian Ming has said about Mr Stanyer.'

Mr Stanyer nodded, but he looked uncomfortable.

'Firstly, that he has been giving her private lessons for money in the school itself, outside of school hours. This is clearly untrue. That would be a very serious matter indeed. Mr Stanyer has told me that he simply wished to give Hu some extra work after class, a very kind and generous offer on his part. Of course, no money was involved.'

Hu's mouth fell open. Hu's father's face didn't change. Mr Grisman hurried on.

'Secondly, she says that Mr Stanyer gave Hu bad results in order to persuade her to take these "private lessons". A very serious matter.' Mr Grisman looked at Hu angrily. 'You are a student, Miss Hu; Mr Stanyer is a teacher, a professional.'

Still Hu's father's face didn't change.

'Thirdly,' Mr Grisman continued, 'that on one occasion Mr Stanyer invited her back to his apartment for further lessons and "to be more comfortable".' Mr Grisman looked at Hu's parents angrily. 'I hope you realise just how serious this is?'

There was a long silence. Hu's father stared back at the school principal. He said nothing.

'And lastly, she says that other female students have been in the same situation. We needn't discuss that. There have been no other complaints.'

There was another long silence.

'Now, Hu Jian Ming,' said Khun Preecha, softly. 'What have you got to say for yourself?' He looked at her in a kind and interested way.

Quietly and with dignity, Hu's father spoke. He looked first at Khun Preecha and then at Mr Grisman.

'Principal, my daughter has told me about the things that happened with Mr Stanyer. I will try to explain her point of view.'

The men on the other side of the table looked at each other. Mr Grisman, Declan Stanyer and David Riding seemed to be smiling. Khun Preecha was not. He turned to look at Hu Jian Ming. His eyes didn't leave hers.

* * *

Verity Truman looked at her watch again. She reached for the phone. 'May I speak to Wiwat Phalavadhana?' she asked. 'Left his office? . . . When? . . . Coming here? . . . No, no. Thank you, thank you.' She replaced the phone. She placed her hands together and made a prayer. 'Please, please don't let the traffic be too bad!'

* * *

Hu's father spoke very well, but the three men facing him didn't seem to believe him. He showed them the book Hu had used to write down the times and money for her private lessons. Suddenly Mr Riding sat forward.

'Principal, may I have that?' Mr Grisman gave it to him. 'Hmph!' He laughed briefly. 'This is pure teenage story telling.' He laughed some more. Mr Riding's laugh was not a happy or a funny laugh.

'It's not unusual for teenage girls to have strong feelings for older men, particularly men in an important position. A teacher perhaps. Hu makes up a story about Mr Stanyer giving her bad results because she doesn't like the truth.

The truth is that her results in English just aren't good enough. And she can't tell her father because she's afraid of him.'

Hu's father showed emotion at last. He went very red in the face.

'And then ...' Mr Riding spoke slowly, smiling. 'And then we have the invitation back to Mr Stanyer's apartment.' He turned and looked at Hu. 'Would you *like* Mr Stanyer to invite you back to his apartment?'

Hu looked at Mr Stanyer. He was smiling back at Mr Riding. She looked at her father. She had never seen him so angry. Khun Preecha was not smiling. He was looking down; she couldn't meet his eyes.

*   *   *

'At last!' said Verity Truman looking up. Wiwat Phalavadhana was standing in the door of her office, holding up his bag. He was a small, bright-eyed man of about forty, well-dressed and with a proud and happy smile.

'I have it, Verity!' he said.

'Let's go!' They hurried out of her office.

*   *   *

'I think we must make a decision,' said Mr Grisman. 'And this is it. Mr Riding has shown that Hu Jian Ming has some very serious problems. I think it is these problems which have led her to say these things about our friend and colleague, Mr Stanyer.' Mr Riding nodded.

Then the door of the principal's office opened.

Chapter 14 *A path to the future*

'Mrs Truman!' said Mr Grisman angrily. 'I am in an important meeting. I . . .' He stopped. He was embarrassed. He didn't want the chair of the school's Board of Governors, Khun Preecha, to see him shouting at his head of Upper School. Then he noticed the person standing behind Verity Truman.

It was Khun Wiwat Phalavadhana. Mr Grisman knew how important he was. Wiwat gave Mr Grisman a very warm smile.

'I . . .' Mr Grisman began again. 'I'm sorry. This is a very important meeting about one of our teachers.'

'That's what we want to talk to you about,' said Verity Truman. 'I think . . . we're sure that what Hu Jian Ming has been saying about Mr Stanyer is true.'

Khun Preecha stared at Mrs Truman. He was listening carefully.

'Surely there must be some misunderstanding,' said Mr Grisman. 'But come in, come in.'

Verity and Wiwat entered the office.

'We don't think so. We don't think Hu has misunderstood at all,' said Verity, opening her bag and bringing out some papers. 'And other people don't think so either. There are other students involved, female students. I've spoken to their parents and some of the students too. Mr Stanyer's little game has been going on for some time . . .'

'Stories, Verity,' said Mr Riding. 'Teenage stories made up by teenage girls. They don't understand their own feelings, they talk together ... Then they make up some story. If one girl tells a story, if six girls tell a story, it's still a story.' He looked at the principal. Mr Grisman looked nervous.

'They're all telling the same story, Mr Riding,' Verity Truman threw the papers down on the table in front of the principal. 'And I've been checking the results of the students Mr Stanyer has been giving "private lessons" to. They all had good results until they came to his class, and the older ones have had good results since they left his class. I think he's been changing the results ... downwards.'

'But Mrs Truman, you're not an English teacher. You are attacking a colleague ...' Mr Grisman was very angry.

'And the girls all tell the story about being invited back to his apartment to be "more comfortable".'

'A story,' said Mr Riding, but he seemed less certain now.

'Perhaps I can speak now?' said Wiwat Phalavadhana, taking some papers from his case. He gave them to Khun Preecha who nodded his head in thanks. The papers were in Thai. 'Mr Stanyer does not have permission to work in Thailand.'

'A small administrative problem, Khun Wiwat. I was not responsible for giving Mr Stanyer the job,' Mr Grisman said.

'Mr Stanyer asked for permission to work in Thailand about three months before he joined the Academy,' Wiwat said. 'He wanted to work for a small private school – Audio English – on Siam Square. There was a problem. I telephoned the director of Audio English. He told me they had checked Mr Stanyer's qualifications back in the USA ...'

Mr Grisman looked at his hands.

'... and found that there was no student called Mr Declan Stanyer at Ohio State University. No record. They didn't believe he was qualified. Since then Mr Stanyer has been coming in and out of Thailand on tourist visas every few months.'

Mr Grisman was shaking his head. 'I was not responsible for giving Mr Stanyer a job. My head of Upper School, Dr Nyondo, gave him the job. But surely it's an administrative problem?' said Mr Grisman, looking at Wiwat.

'It's the law, Mr Grisman,' said Khun Preecha, quietly.

'And I think you'd better see these,' said Verity. She handed Mr Grisman a large brown envelope. 'I found them in Mr Stanyer's desk drawer.'

'You've been looking in the drawer of his desk, Mrs Truman?' Mr Grisman was shocked. He took the envelope and pulled out a pile of magazines.

Mr Grisman was silent for a moment. His face went white. Everyone was looking at him as he looked at the magazines. He opened one of the magazines and shut it again quickly. He shut his eyes. Then he stood up. He screamed:

'*Mr Stanyer!*'

But Mr Stanyer wasn't there. His chair was empty. The door of the principal's office was open.

Mr Stanyer had left them.

Chapter 15 *The right career*

Hu found her parents standing outside the school hall with Verity Truman and the principal, Mr Grisman. It was a warm night. The summer was coming. Hu was still wearing her make up and her costume, her special clothes as Dorothy. Hu felt wonderful, the show was a success!

As she came closer to the group of adults, she could see that Mr Grisman was talking very quickly and waving his arms.

'Just disappeared! Three weeks now, and no-one's seen him. Of course the police are still interested. But I had no idea! I was away when he was given the job. The head of Upper School then, Mr Nyondo, had made the arrangements. And of course, the school will pay back the money Hu spent on the, er …' Mr Grisman laughed nervously. 'The "private lessons". But your daughter was wonderful, wonderful. A Chinese Dorothy!' Mr Grisman seemed to find this very funny.

'Wonderful!' said Verity Truman, taking Hu's arm and smiling warmly.

Sean and Thomas joined the group. Sean was also still in costume and make up.

'Sean, you were wonderful!' shouted Verity.

Everyone was talking at once. John Truman and his sister, Mary, joined them. Marwa and Yoshiko joined the group. They all told Hu and Sean how wonderful the show had been.

'Hu, I'd like you to meet someone,' said Verity.

A tall Thai woman in a lovely silk dress came over and joined the group. Hu's mother admired the woman's dress. Hu's father simply stared. Hu was embarrassed.

'This is Dr Irene, Director of the Bangkok Operatic Society,' said Verity.

'Is this the star? Hu Jian Ming?' said Dr Irene. 'I thought your performance was wonderful, Hu. You sing beautifully. Have you had any training?' Hu introduced Dr Irene to her mother. They soon began talking about opera together.

Hu took the opportunity to speak to Thomas. She hadn't seen him since the Khao Yai field trip because he had been in hospital.

'Thomas, I'm sorry you couldn't be in the show,' said Hu. 'Are you OK now?'

'Yes, thanks to him,' said Thomas. He pretended to hit Sean. Sean pretended to fall over. 'I don't like hospital. Too many doctors.'

Hu's mother came towards them.

'Dr Irene wants you to sing with the Operatic Society, Hu,' Hu's mother said in an excited voice. 'And she's a professional singer!'

'I'm a semi-professional singer,' said Dr Irene. 'I'm a professional doctor.'

'She's the senior doctor at the Pattana Clinic, Hu,' said Hu's father. He was full of pride for his daughter. 'She wants you to sing in their new show.'

'Do you like Mozart, Hu?' asked Doctor Irene. 'Our next show at the Operatic Society is a Mozart opera.'

Hu looked at Dr Irene.

'Well?' said Dr Irene.

Then Hu looked at her father.

'A singer and a doctor?' she said to her father, smiling. 'Or a doctor and a singer?'

Her father just smiled, and smiled.

3 . . 12245